BEANS

Bootstrap ExpressJS AngularJS NodeJS Sock
How to Write Real-time Features in JavaScript.
by Brendon Co

ISBN-13: 978-1502541147
ISBN-10: 1502541149

Cover Image by Brendon Co

About the Author

Brendon Co is a programmer and entrepreneur who have a passion for JavaScript programming language. He's the creator and lead developer of Movie R Us Internet video streaming for mobile devices and lead developer on many web-based, mobile and desktop development projects. He was the author of Learning AngulasJS the Easy Way (Link: http://www.amazon.com/dp/B00IT9QCFQ).

Acknowledgements

The author has adapted portions of this book from previously release title, Learning AngularJS the Easy Way.

I'd like to take this opportunity to thank everyone who made this book possible. It was a tremendous amount of work, and I appreciate all the help and guidance that I received along the way.

I would like to thank my family and friends for supporting me and encouraging me throughout the years.

I am very grateful for the readers who provided comments and I owe them much in correcting my errors and improving my writing.

Welcome to NodeJS

Node.js is a platform built on Chrome's JavaScript runtime for easy building fast, scalable network applications. Node.js uses an event-driven, non-blocking I/O model that makes it lightweight and efficient, perfect for data-intensive real-time applications that run across distributed devices.

For newcomers to Node.js, Node is not a webserver. By itself it doesn't do anything. It doesn't work like Apache Tomcat. There is no config file where you point it to your HTML files. If you want it to behave like an HTTP server, you have to write an HTTP server (with the help of its built-in libraries). Node.js is another way to execute JavaScript code on your computer. It is simply a JavaScript runtime.

Installation and Guide

In preparation for building Node application I thought it would be a good idea to help you get started by setting up your environment.

Recommended platform is *nix operating system.

Step 1: A Posix OS

If you are not using Windows, proceed to Step 2.

If you are using Windows, go get a Cygwin and install it. Instructions are available below (Building Node.js on Cygwin Windows).

Building Node.js on Cygwin Windows:
https://github.com/joyent/node/wiki/Building-node.js-on-Cygwin-%28Windows%29

npm (Node Packaged Modules) – is the official package manager for Node.js. As of Node.js version 0.6.3, npm is bundled and installed automatically with the environment. npm runs through the command line and manages dependencies for an application.

> **Important:** Make sure you follow ALL the steps! It'll seem like it's working before you get to the end. But it is a dirty, lying liar. Don't believe it. Do the steps all the way to the end. If you don't, you're going to complain that npm says "ECONNREFUSED" and then post a bug, and Node.js developer will ask you whether you did all the steps, and you'll feel silly.

Step 2: Compiler

If you are using any kind of Linux or Unix system. Just skip ahead to Step 3.

Mac users go and install Xcode, if you haven't.

(ProTip: It's on the OS X install CD if you don't want to wait for the giant download)

Get Xcode:
http://developer.apple.com/technologies/tools/xcode.html

Step 3: Terminal

Download the Node.js pre-built installer for your platform.

Pre-built installer:
http://nodejs.org/download/

Installation Guide:
https://github.com/joyent/node/wiki/Installation

```
$ wget http://nodejs.org/dist/v0.10.31/node-v0.10.31.tar.gz

$ tar —xzf node-v0.10.31.tar.gz

$ cd node-v0.10.31.gz

$ ./configure

$ sudo make install
```

On OSX you must install XCode for this to work.

On Ubuntu you probably have to run:
$ apt-get —y install build-essential

To check if Node.js is installed, in command prompt or terminal, type node –v. This will show you what version of Node.js installed on your machine e.g. v0.10.xx.

Installing without building

You may obtain pre-compiled Node.js binaries for several platforms from http://nodejs.org/download.

Writing NodeJS

I've installed Node, now what?

Once installed you'll have access to a new command called "node". You can use the node command in two different ways. The first is with no arguments. This will open an interactive shell (REPL: read-eval-print-loop) where you can execute raw JavaScript code.

```
$ node
> console.log('Hello World');
Hello World
undefined
```

In the above example I typed node with no arguments and hit enter. I typed "console.log('Hello World');" into shell and hit enter again. Node will then execute that code and we can see our logged message. It also prints "undefined" because it displays the return value of each command and console.log doesn't return anything.

The other way to run Node is by providing an argument a JavaScript file to execute. This is almost always how you'll be using it.

HelloWorld.js

Writing a node.js program is as simple as creating a new javascript file with a '.js' extension. For example, create 'HelloWorld.js' file with the following content:

```
console.log('Hello World');
```

After you have saved the file, you can execute it from your terminal like so:

```
$ node HelloWorld.js
Hello World
```

Listening to port 8080 and Response Hello World

Make sure you don't have other web server that listen to port 8080. If you have, please use other port number or shutdown that server. For this tutorial, we'll be using port 8080.

Printing Hello World to a terminal isn't exciting at all. Let's take the next step and write a program that listen to port 8080 and responds Hello World via http. We'll call the file 'Http_HelloWorld.js' and put the following code:

```
var http = require('http');

var server = http.createServer(
function(request, response) {
  response.writeHead(200);
  response.end('Hello World');
});

server.listen(8080);
```

Now lets run this program from the terminal by typing:

```
$ node Http_HelloWorld.js
```

The first thing you'll notice is that this program, unlike our HelloWorld.js, doesn't exit right away. That's because a node program will always run until it's certain that no further events are possible. In this case the open http server is the source of events that will keep things going.

There are many ways to test the server. Open a new browser and navigating to the following url: http://localhost:8080/. As expected, you should see a response that reads: 'Hello World'.

Alternatively, you could also open up a terminal and use curl to test your server:

```
$ curl http://localhost:8080/
Hello World
```

Now let's have a closer look at the steps involved in our program. In the first line, we include the http core module and assign it to a variable called http. You will find more information on this in the next section about the module system.

Next we create a variable called server by calling a function in http called http.createServer. The argument passed into this call is a closure that is called whenever an http request comes in.

Note: Closures are functions that refer to independent (free) variables.

In other words, function defined in the closure 'remembers' the environement in which it was created.

To learn more about closure:
http://www.w3schools.com/js/js_function_closures.asp

Finally we call a function server.listen(8080) to inform node.js the port on which we want our server to listen.

Now when you access 'localhost:8080' in your browser, the connection closure is invoked with a request and response object. The request is a readable stream that emits data events for each incoming request of data e.g. form submission. The response object is a writable stream that is used to output or send data back to the client. In our case we are simply sending a 200 OK header, as we as the body 'Hello World'.

Module Loader

Using a modular script loader will improve the speed and quality of your code. Node.js provides you with a simple module system and structure your program into different files.

Let's create a new file called 'main.js' with the following content. Below illustrate the approach:

```
var hello = require('./helloworld'); hello.world();
```

The require('./helloworld') is used to import the contents from another JavaScript file. The './' indicates that the file is located in the same directory as 'main.js'. Take note that you don't have to provide the file extension, '.js' is assumed by default.

Let's create 'helloworld.js', with the following content:

```
exports.hw = function() {
    console.log('Hello World');
};
```

Notice above, that we are assigning a property called 'hw' to an object call 'exports'. Such an 'exports' object is available in every module, and it is returned whenever the require function is used to include the module. When we run our 'main.js', we expect to see the output below:

```
$ node main.js
Hello World
```

Many node users are overwriting the exports object directly:

```
Module.exports = function(){
// . . .
};
```

You might have guessed it, this will directly cause the require function to return the assigned function. This is useful if you're doing object oriented programming where each file exports the constructor of one class.

How Module System deals with require:

What node will do, is to first look if there is a core module name and if there is, return that directly. Take for example:

```
var http = require('http');
```

But what about non-core modules, such as 'jquery' or 'mysql'?

```
$ = require('jquery');
```

Or

```
var mysql = require('mysql');
```

In this case node.js will look up the directory tree, moving through each parent directory, checking in each to see if there is a folder called 'node_modules'. If such a folder is found, node.js will look into this folder for a file called 'jquery.js' or 'mysql.js'. If no matching file is found and the root directory '/' is reached, node.js will throw an exception.

EventEmitters:

Node.js implements the observer pattern called EventEmitters.

Using EventEmitters is pretty much straight forward. You can listen to an event by calling 'on()' function on your object, providing the name of the event, as well as callback closure as the parameters. For example:

```
var data ='';
request.on('data',function(value){
   data += value;
}).on('end', function(){
   console.log('POST data: %s', data);
});
```

The above example, the 'on()' function also returns a reference to the object it belongs to, allowing you to chain several of such event listeners.

If you're interested in the first occurrence of an event, you can use the 'once()' function instead.

You can remove event listeners by using 'removeListener' function. Please note that the argument to this function is a reference to the callback you are trying to remove, not the name of the event.

```
var onData = function(value){
  console.log(value);
  request.removeListener(onData);
};

request.on('data', onData);
```

The example above is identical to 'once()' function.

Now that you know the basics of Node.js, you probably want to try to experiment a few programs by yourself. You can find more about Node.js API documentation:

Link: http://nodejs.org/docs/v0.4.4/api/

Debugging Node.js
There are a lot of ways to debug your node.js applications. But I prefer to write a test driven development.

However, if you find yourself in a situation where you are scratching your head and want to locate a tricky bug in an existing application, here are a few ways that can help.

Using node debugger

If you think that your problem can be better analyzed using breakpoints, node's built-in debugger is a great choice. You can invoke the debugger by simply using below syntax:

```
$ node debug yourfile.js
< debugger listening on port 5858
connecting... ok
break in yourfile.js:3
1 var s = "My String";
2 setTimeout(function(){
3   debugger;
debug>
```

Node's debugger client doesn't support full range of commands, but simple step and inspection is possible. By putting the statement 'debugger;' into the source code of your script, you will enable a breakpoint.

For example, suppose yourfile.js looked like this:

```
1   //yourfile.js
2   var x = "My String";
3   setTimeout(function(){
4     debugger;
5     console.log("world");
6   }, 1000);
7   console.log("Hello");
```

Then once the debugger is run, it will break on line 4.

```
$ node debug yourfile.js
< debugger listening on port 5858
connecting... ok
break in yourfile.js:2
  1 // yourfile.js
  2 x = "My String";
  3 setTimeout(function () {
  4   debugger;
debug> cont
```

```
< hello
break in yourfile.js:4
  2 x = "My String";
  3 setTimeout(function () {
  4    debugger;
  5    console.log("world");
  6 }, 1000);
debug> next
break in yourfile.js:5
  3 setTimeout(function () {
  4    debugger;
  5    console.log("world");
  6 }, 1000);
  7 console.log("Hello");
Press Ctrl + C to leave debug repl
> x
'My String'
>
```

The 'repl' command allows you to evaluate code remotely. The
'next' command steps over to the next line. Type 'help'
command to see other commands available.

Visit the link below to know more about Node debugger:

http://nodejs.org/api/debugger.html

Using console.log()
If you want to understand your problem by inspecting objects
using console.log(). You can directly pass in objects as
parameters:

```
var f = {name: 'George'};
console.log(f);
```

Or you can pass a format specifiers, a string token composed of
the percent sign (%) followed by a letter that indicates the
formatting to be applied:

```
var f = {name: 'George'};
console.log('Hi %s, my object: %j', f.name, f);
```

Simple Chat Messenger

In this guide we'll create a simple chat messenger application using ExpressJS and Socket.io modules. The server can push messages to all other connected clients whenever you write a message.

Create package.json

```json
{
    "name": "SampleMessenger",
    "version": "1.0.0",
    "description": "Sample Messenger with socket.io and express",
    "dependencies": {},
    "author": "Brendon Co"
}
```

Using ExpressJS

Install express as dependecies in our project. We'll use npm install express --save. This will populate the dependencies in package.json file.

Type the following command below to install express:

```
$ npm install express --save
```

Now that express is installed we can create server.js file and setup our application.

```
1  var express = require('express');
2  var appHttp = require('http');
3
4  var MessengerApi = function(){
5  var self = this;
6
7  self.init = function(){
8
9    self.app = express();
10
11   self.app.use(express.static(__dirname + '/public'));
```

```
12    self.http = appHttp.Server(self.app);
13 }//End of self.init function
14
15 self.startApp = function(){
16    self.init();
17
18    self.http.listen(3000, function(){
19       console.log('listening on : 3000');
20    });
21 }
22 }; // end of MessengerApi function
23
24 var s = new MessengerApi();
25 s.startApp();
```

The codes above can be translated into the following:

1. Express initializes 'self.app' to be a function handler as shown in line 9. It can be supplied to an HTTP server (as seen in line 12).

2. In line 11, we mount the middleware function at the path. __dirname is the name of the directory that the currently executing script resides in. The 'public' is a folder we created in our project, hence this is where we place our 'index.html' file, and it contains the chat client. We'll discuss it in next section.

3. In line 18, we make the server listen to port '3000'.

4. In line 24, we initialize our MessengerApi by using 'new' keyword.

5. In line 25, we start our application.

Using Socket.io

Socket.io is composed of two parts:

- A server that integrates with the Node.JS HTTP Server: socket.io

- A client library that loads on the browser side: socket.io.client

We don't need to install socket.io.client. socket.io serves the client automatically, hence we only have to install one module.

Install socket.io as dependencies in our project. We'll use npm install socket.io --save. This will populate the dependencies in package.json file.

```
$ npm install socket.io --save
```

Type the following command below to install socket.io:

Server:

Now let's edit 'server.js' and add socket.io.

```
1 'use strict';
2
3 var express = require('express');
4 var appHttp = require('http');
5 var server = require('socket.io');
6
7 var MessengerApi = function(){
8   var self = this;
9
10   self.init = function(){
11
12     self.app = express();
13
14     //For socket.io.client to work
15     //pointing to static public/index.html
16     self.app.use(express.static(__dirname + '/public'));
17
18     self.http = appHttp.Server(self.app);
19
20     //For socket.io.client to work
21     self.io = server(appHttp);
22 }
23
24   self.startApp = function(){
25     self.init();
26
27     //For socket.io.client to work
28     //Assigned the
29     self.appServer = self.http.listen(3000, function(){
30       console.log('listening on : 3000');
31     });
32
33       self.startServerMessenger();
34 }
```

```
35
36    self.startServerMessenger = function(){
37    var CONNECTION = 'connection';
38
39    //For socket.io.client to work
40    //io.listen should be passed an http.Server instance,
41    //hence http.Server instance returned by self.http.listen
42    self.socket = self.io.listen(self.appServer);
43
44    self.socket.on(CONNECTION, function(socket){
45        console.log('a user connected');
46      });
47    }
48  };
49
50  var s = new MessengerApi();
51  s.startApp();
```

The codes above can be translated into the following:

1. In line 16, I use a middleware to serve the content from
    a public directory. In this case the 'public' directory is
    served up and any content (HTML, CSS, JavaScript) will
    be available. This means if the public directory looks
    like the following:

    1. index.html

    2. js/app.js

    Then you can request the root route '/' you'll get
    index.html file and if 'js/app.js' is requested you receive
    the app.js file in the js folder. This is all to be expected
    from a static server.

2. In line 21, I initialize a new instance of socket.io by
    passing the appHttp (HTTP server) object.

3. In line 44, I listen on 'connection' event for incoming
    sockets, and log it into the console.

Create public/index.html

Create a 'public' directory and place 'index.html' file into
the 'public' directory. The content of index.html looks like
below.

```
 1  <!doctype html>
 2  <html>
 3    <head>
 4      <title>Socket.IO chat</title>
 5      <style>
 6        * { margin: 0; padding: 0; box-sizing: border-box; }
 7        body { font: 13px Helvetica, Arial; }
 8        form { background: #000; padding: 3px; position: fixed; bottom:
0; width: 100%; }
 9        form input { border: 0; padding: 10px; width: 90%; margin-right:
.5%; }
10        form button { width: 9%; background: rgb(130, 224, 255); border:
none; padding: 10px; }
11        #messages { list-style-type: none; margin: 0; padding: 0; }
12        #messages li { padding: 5px 10px; }
13        #messages li:nth-child(odd) { background: #eee; }
14      </style>
15    </head>
16    <body>
17      <script src="./socket.io/socket.io.js"></script>
18      <script>
19        var socket = io();
20      </script>
21    </body>
22  </html>
```

Notice in index.html I add the following snippet before the
closing body tag </body>

```
<script src="./socket.io/socket.io.js"></script>
<script>
  var socket = io();
</script>
```

The above snippets load the socket.io-client, which
expose 'io' global, and then connect to the server.

Notice I didn't specify any URL when I call io(), since it
defaults to trying to connect to the host that serves the
page.

If you run node server.js you should see the following:

```
$ node server.js
listening on : 3000
```

And if you point your browser to http://localhost:3000/,

You should see below snapshot.

If you reload the server and the website you should see the console print "a user connected". Try opening several tabs, and you'll see several messages displayed at the console.

```
$ node server.js
listening on : 3000
a user connected
a user connected
```

Each socket also fires special disconnect event. In server.js, add a new event that listen to disconnect event.

```
self.socket.on(CONNECTION, function(socket){
    console.log('a user connected');

    socket.on('disconnect', function(){
        console.log('user disconnected');
    });

});
```

Then if you refresh a tab several times you can see it in action:

```
$ node server.js
listening on : 3000
a user connected
user disconnected
a user connected
```

Using AngularJS + Socket.IO:

AngularJS is a great JavaScript framework that gives you two- way data binding that's easy to use and fast, a powerful directive system that let's you create reusable custom components, plus a lot more. Socket.IO is a cross-browser wrapper and polyfill for websockets that makes developing real-time applications a breeze. I find the two work quite well together!

I've written before about Learning AngularJS the Easy Way(Link: http://www.amazon.com/dp/B00IT9QCFQ), but this time I'll be writing about how to integrate Socket.IO to add real-time features to an AngularJS application. In this tutorial, I'm going to walk you through writing an instant messaging application.

You can get the finished project on Github.

Link:

https://github.com/brendonco/samplemessenger

Socket.IO Emitting Events:

You can use Socket.IO to send and receive any events you want, with any data you want. You can encode an object into JSON or binary data.

Let's create a JavaScript file called app.js and include our logic, so that when the user types in a message, the server gets it as a chat message event.

Create js/app.js

```
1 (function(ng){
 2
 3 var SEND_MSG = 'send:message';
 4 var INIT = 'init';
 5 var CHANGE_NAME = 'change:name';
 6 var USER_JOIN = 'user:join';
 7 var USER_LEFT = 'user:left';
 8 var CHAT_ROOM = 'chatroom';
 9 var ERR_CHANGING_NAME = 'There was an error changing your name';
10
11 var app = ng.module('app', ['services', 'custom-filters']);
12
13 app.controller('FormController', ['$scope', 'socket', function($scope,
socket){
14    $scope.message = "";
15    $scope.messages = [];
16    $scope.friends = [];
17
18    //Initialize Socket listeners
19    socket.on(INIT, function(data){
20      $scope.name = data.name;
21      $scope.friends = data.friends;
22    });
23
24    socket.on(SEND_MSG, function(msg){
25      $scope.messages.push(msg);
26    });
27
28    socket.on(CHANGE_NAME, function(data){
29      changeName(data.prevName, data.currentName);
30    });
31
32    socket.on(USER_JOIN, function(data){
33      $scope.messages.push({
34        user: CHAT_ROOM,
35        text: 'User ' + data.name + ' has joined.'
36      });
37
38      $scope.friends.push(data.name);
39    });
40
41    //Add a message to the conversation when a user is disconnected or
leaves the chat room.
42    socket.on(USER_LEFT, function(data){
43      $scope.messages.push({
44        user: CHAT_ROOM,
45        text: 'User ' + data.name + ' has left.'
46      });
47
48      var i=0; var friend='';
49
50      for(i; i < $scope.friends.length; i++){
51        friend = $scope.friends[i]
```

```
52
53          if(friend === data.name){
54            $scope.friends.splice(i, 1);
55            break;
56          }
57        }
58    });
59
60    var changeName = function(prevName, currentName){
61      var i=0;
62
63      for(i; i < $scope.users.length; i++){
64        if($scope.friends[i] === prevName){
65          $scope.friends[i] = currentName;
66          break;
67        }
68      }
69
70      $scope.messages.push({
71        user: CHAT_ROOM,
72        text: 'User ' + prevName + ' is now known as ' + currentName +
'.'
73      });
74    }
75
76    $scope.changeName = function(){
77      socket.emit(CHANGE_NAME, {
78        name: $scope.currentName
79      }, function(result){
80        if(!result){
81          alert(ERR_CHANGING_NAME);
82        }else{
83          changeName($scope.name, $scope.currentName);
84
85          $scope.name = $scope.currentName;
86          $scope.currentName = '';
87        }
88      });
89    }
90
91    $scope.submit = function(){
92      socket.emit(SEND_MSG, {msg: $scope.message});
93
94      $scope.messages.push({
95          user: $scope.name,
96          text: $scope.message
97      });
98
99      $scope.message = "";
100   }
101 }]);
102
103 })(angular);
```

Interacting with Socket.IO

Although Socket.IO exposes an io variable on the window, it's better to encapsulate it in AngularJS's Dependency Injection system(http://docs.angularjs.org/guide/di). So, we'll write a service to wrap the socket object returned by Socket.IO. This will make it much easier to test our controller later.

js/services/services.js

```
 1 function(ng){
 2     "use strict";
 3
 4     var app = ng.module('services', []);
 5
 6     app.factory('socket', ['$rootScope', function($rootScope){
 7         var socket = io.connect();
 8         return {
 9             on: function (eventName, callback) {
10                 socket.on(eventName, function () {
11                     var args = arguments;
12                     $rootScope.$apply(function () {
13                         callback.apply(socket, args);
14                     });
15                 });
16             },
17             emit: function (eventName, data, callback) {
18                 socket.emit(eventName, data, function () {
19                     var args = arguments;
20                     $rootScope.$apply(function () {
21                         if (callback) {
22                             callback.apply(socket, args);
23                         }
24                     });
25                 })
26             }
27         };
28     }]);
29
30 })(angular);
```

Notice that we wrap each socket callback in $scope.$apply. This tells AngularJS that it needs to check the state of the application and update the templates if there was change after running the callback passed to it.

Note that this service doesn't wrap the entire Socket.IO. However, it covers the methods used in this book.

Custom AngularJS Filter

Customize filter to display the current user at the top of the user list.

Let's create a filter file called filters.js and include our logic, so that when you join the chat room, you will always see your username at the top of the user list.

Create js/filters/filters.js:

```
1  (function(ng){
2      "use strict";
3
4      var app = ng.module('custom-filters', []);
5
6      /*
7       * Customize filter to display the current user at the top of the
user list.
8       */
9      app.filter('moveCurrentUserToTop', [function(){
10         return function(friends, name){
11             var newList = [];
12
13             ng.forEach(friends, function(u){
14                 if(u === name){
15                     newList.unshift(u);
16                 }else{
17                     newList.push(u);
18                 }
19             });
20
21             return newList;
22         }
23     }]);
24 })(angular);
```

The codes above can be translated into the following:

1. In line 4 we defined a module name for our filter.

2. In line 9 we defined a filter name called 'moveCurrentUserToTop'.

3. In line 13 to 19 we iterate the friends array and compare the username. If it is a new user, we add it at the top of the user list; otherwise we push it at the end of the array and return the new array.

How to use custom filter:

Modify index.html and add the code snippets below after "user-chat-msg" unordered HTML list (<ul class="user-chat-msg"></ul>).

```
    <ul class="users">
        <li ng-repeat="friend in friends | moveCurrentUserToTop: name" ng-
class="{'current-user': name === friend}">
            <span ng-if="friend === name">{{friend}} (me)</span>
            <span ng-if="friend !== name">{{friend}}</span>
        </li>
    </ul>
```

The codes above can be translated into the following:

1. We are passing the new username into our custom filter "moveCurrentUserToTop" so that we can compare it and move it to the top of the user list.

2. I want to modify the username and add "(me)", so that if I don't want to change the username, I can still identify myself in the user list.

Visit below link to know more about AngularJS Filter:

Link: "https://docs.angularjs.org/api/ng/filter/filter".

Bootstrap + AngularJS

Dependencies:

- Jquery
- Bootstrap
- AngularJS

Download the dependency files or use CDN hosted by respective vendors.

Links:

1. Jquery: http://jquery.com/download/
2. Bootstrap: http://getbootstrap.com/getting-started/
3. AngularJS: https://docs.angularjs.org/misc/downloading

Bootstrap + AngularJS + JQuery CDN:

For this tutorial, we'll be using these links provided by the respective vendors through CDN.

```
<link rel="stylesheet"
href="https://maxcdn.bootstrapcdn.com/bootstrap/3.2.0/css/bootstrap.min.css
">

<script
src="//ajax.googleapis.com/ajax/libs/jquery/1.9.0/jquery.min.js"></script>
    <!-- Latest compiled and minified JavaScript -->

<script
src="https://maxcdn.bootstrapcdn.com/bootstrap/3.2.0/js/bootstrap.min.js"><
/script>

<script
src="https://ajax.googleapis.com/ajax/libs/angularjs/1.2.0/angular.min.js">
</script>
```

Customize Dialog using AngularJS Directives:

Let's use bootstrap modal and AngularJS directive to create the dialog. One common need I have is to be able to show or hide Bootstrap modal based on a property on my view-model.

```
1  (function(ng){
2    "use strict";
3
4    var app = ng.module('dialog', []);
5
6    app.directive('popupWindow', [function(){
7      return {
8        restrict: 'E',
9        replace: true,
10       link: function(scope, element, attr){
11         scope.hideModal = function(){
12           element.modal('hide');
13         };
14
15         scope.showModal = function(){
16           element.modal('show');
17         };
18       },
19       templateUrl: '../html/dialog/dialog.html'
20     };
21   }]);
22 })(angular);
```

The codes above can be translated into the following:

1. Line 12 and 16, we are calling Bootstrap method modal on the element to which the directive is applied to show or hide the dialog.

2. Also note that we didn't defined controller in our "popupWindow" directive, since we are going to reuse the same controller "FormController".

Note: You can customize the "popupWindow" directive and make it more reusable by using isolating the scope.

Dialog HTML template:

```
1  <div class="modal fade" id="form-content" tabindex="-1" role="dialog"
   aria-labelledby="myModalLabel" aria-hidden="true">
2
3       <div class="modal-dialog">
4           <div class="modal-content">
5               <div class="modal-header">
6                   <button type="button" class="close" data-
   dismiss="modal"><span aria-hidden="true">&times;</span><span class="sr-
   only">Close</span></button>
7                   <h4 class="modal-title" id="myModalLabel">Change your
   name</h4>
8               </div>
9               <div class="modal-body">
10                  <span>Your current username is {{name}}</span>
11                  <form action="" ng-submit="changeName()">
12                      <div>
13                          <input name="name" type="text" ng-
   model="friend.name"/>
14                      </div>
15                  </form>
16              </div>
17              <div class="modal-footer">
18                  <button type="button" class="btn btn-default" data-
   dismiss="modal">Close</button>
19                  <button type="button" class="btn btn-primary" ng-
   click="changeName()">Save changes</button>
20              </div>
21          </div>
22      </div>
23 </div>
```

The codes above can be translated into the following:

1. In line 9, the form tag must be after "modal-body" class.

2. In line 10, we show the current username by using AngularJS expression. Visit AngularJS to know more about expression.

   Link:

   https://docs.angularjs.org/guide/expression

3. In line 11, we use ngSubmit directive to call the "changeName" function when submitting the form. The user may press "ENTER" key or click the "Save changes" button to submit the form.

4. In line 13, we use ngModel directive to bind an input to a property on the scope e.g. "friend.name".

5. In line 6 and 18, we use bootstrap markup "data-dismiss" to the close button.

To know more about AngularJS Directives visit below link:

Link: https://docs.angularjs.org/guide/directive

Writing the Server

Let's reuse and modify our previous Node.js applicaton.

First, create a new file called "friends.js". We need to define an object for maintaining the state of the server, so that the names are unique.

```
1 var friends = {};
2 friends.names = {};
3
4 friends.claim = function(name){
5     if(!name || friends.names[name]){
6         return false;
7     }else{
8         friends.names[name] = true;
9         return true;
10    }
11 }
12
13 /*
14 * Use LRU pattern to find unused guest name and claim it.
15 **/
16 friends.getGuestName = function(){
17     var name; var nextUserId = 1;
18
19     do{
20         name = 'Guest ' + nextUserId;
21         nextUserId += 1;
22     }while(!friends.claim(name));
23
24     return name;
25 }
26
27 /**
28 * Serialize claimed names.
29 */
30 friends.getFriends = function(){
31     var names = [];
32     var name;
33
34     for(name in friends.names){
35         names.push(name);
36     }
37
38     return names;
39 }
40
41 /**
42 * Delete friend.
43 */
44 friends.removeFriend = function(name){
45     if(friends.names[name]){
46         delete friends.names[name];
47     }
48 }
49
50 module.exports = friends;
```

This basically defines a set of names, but with APIs that make more sense for the domain of a chat server. Let's hook this up to the server's socket to respond to the calls that our client makes. Open and modify "server.js":

```
 1  'use strict';
 2
 3  var express = require('express');
 4  var appHttp = require('http');
 5  var server = require('socket.io');
 6  var userNames = require('./friends');
 7
 8  var MessengerApi = function(){
 9      var self = this;
10
11      self.init = function(){
12          // self.createRoutes();
13          self.app = express();
14
15          //For socket.io.client to work
16          //pointing to static public/index.html
17          self.app.use(express.static(__dirname + '/public/dist'));
18
19          self.http = appHttp.Server(self.app);
20
21          //For socket.io.client to work
22          self.io = server(appHttp);
23      }
24
25      self.startApp = function(){
26          self.init();
27
28          //For socket.io.client to work
29          //Assigned the
30          self.appServer = self.http.listen(3000, function(){
31              console.log('listening on : 3000');
32          });
33
34          self.startServerMessenger();
35      }
36
37      self.startServerMessenger = function(){
38          var CONNECTION = 'connection';
39          var DISCONNECT = 'disconnect';
40
41          var SEND_MSG = 'send:message';
42          var INIT = 'init';
43          var CHANGE_NAME = 'change:name';
44          var USER_JOIN = 'user:join';
45          var USER_LEFT = 'user:left';
46          var CHAT_ROOM = 'chatroom';
47
48          //For socket.io.client to work
49          //io.listen should be passed an http.Server instance,
50          //hence http.Server instance returned by self.http.listen
51          self.socket = self.io.listen(self.appServer);
52
53          self.socket.on(CONNECTION, function(socket){
54              console.log('a user connected');
55
56              var name = userNames.getGuestName();
57
58              //send the new user their name and a list of friends
59              socket.emit(INIT, {name: name, friends:
userNames.getFriends()});
60
61              //notify other clients that a new user has joined
62              socket.broadcast.emit(USER_JOIN, {name: name});
63
64              //broadcast a user's message to other users
65              socket.on(SEND_MSG, function(data){
66                  socket.broadcast.emit(SEND_MSG, {user: name, text:
data.msg});
67              });
```

```
68
69              //validate a user's name change, and broadcast it on
success
70              socket.on(CHANGE_NAME, function(data, fn){
71                  console.log("prepare to change name " + data.name);
72                  if(userNames.claim(data.name)){
73                      var prevName = name;
74
75                      userNames.removeFriend(prevName);
76
77                      name = data.name;
78
79                      console.log(CHANGE_NAME + " prev name: " + prevName
+ " new name: " + name);
80
81                      socket.broadcast.emit(CHANGE_NAME,{prevName:
prevName, currentName: name});
82
83                      fn(true);
84                  }else{
85                      fn(false);
86                  }
87              });
88
89              socket.on(DISCONNECT, function(){
90                  console.log('user ' + name + ' has left.');
91
92                  socket.broadcast.emit(USER_LEFT, {name: name});
93
94                  userNames.removeFriend(name);
95              });
96          });
97      }
98 };
99
100 var s = new MessengerApi();
101 s.startApp();
```

The codes above can be translated into the following:

1. In line 6, we load a module dependency that we created earlier.

2. In line 17, we specify the path were the client reside.

3. In line 51, http listener should be passed an http.Server instance to socket io.

4. In line 53, once the connections are established, the client can send the events same as the events defined in line 59 to line 56.

5. In line 100, we instantiate MessengerApi.

6. In line 101, we run the function startApp defined in line 25.

The project can be downloaded from Github:
http://github.com/brendonco/simplechatserver.

Unit Testing(TDD/BDD):

Installing Mocha and create test folder

```
$ npm install –g mocha
$ mkdir test
```

Refer to Mocha installation guide at:
http://visionmedia.github.io/mocha/#installation

Testing Socket Client:

Installing socket.io-client module

```
$ npm install socket.io-client
```

Create test specification
Make directory called 'test'.

Create a test specification file called 'chat-spec.js' and
save it into test directory.

Broadcast that a new user has joined

Within the describe function (line 16) we will add our first
test that determines if the chat server notifies all users
that a new user has joined.

```
 1 var assert = require("assert");
 2 var io = require('socket.io-client');
 3
 4 var options ={
 5   transports: ['websocket'],
 6   'force new connection': true
 7 };
 8
 9 var url = "http://localhost:3000";
10
11 var chatUser1 = {
12   user: 'chatroom',
13   text: 'User has joined.'
14 };
15
16 describe('Sample Messenger Test', function(){
17     it('Broadcast user to all users', function(done){
18         var client1 = io.connect(url, options);
19
20         client1.on('connect', function(data){
21           client1.emit('user:join', chatUser1);
22
23           done();
24         });
25     });
```

Now that our first test is complete, let's run the server.

```
$ node server.js
listening on : 3000
```

In another terminal window we can run the test.

```
$ mocha
```

Test Result

```
Sample Messenger Test
    ✓ Broadcast user to all users

  1 passing (31ms)
```

Broadcast messages to the whole group
Now we'll add the second test that determines if a message
sent from one client is sent to all clients connected to the chat
server. To determine if all clients have received a message, I
added assert and check the object return by the chat server.
The message that a client sent to the server must be the same
message sent across all clients connected to the chat server
(Refer to line 35).

```
28    it('Broadcast messages to the whole group', function(done){
29      var client1, client2, client3;
30
31      var message = {msg: 'Hello World'};
32
33      var checkMsg = function(client){
34        client.on('send:message', function(msg){
35          assert.equal(message.msg, msg.text);
36
37          client.disconnect();
38        });
39      };
40
41      client1 = io.connect(url, options);
42      checkMsg(client1);
43
44      client1.on('connect', function(data){
45        client2 = io.connect(url, options);
46        checkMsg(client2);
47
48        client2.on('connect', function(data){
49          client3 = io.connect(url, options);
50          checkMsg(client3);
51
52          client3.on('connect', function(data){
53            client2.emit('send:message', message);
54
55            done();
56          });
57        });
58      });
59    });
```

Now that our second test is complete, let's run the server.

```
$ node server.js
listening on : 3000
```

In another terminal window we can run the test.

```
$ mocha
```

Test Result

```
Sample Messenger Test
    ✓ Broadcast user to all users (105ms)
    ✓ Broadcast messages to the whole group


  2 passing (171ms)
```

Conclusion:

There are a lot you could add in this chat messenger application. For instance, you could let the server keep a recent history of messages for the benefit of new users joining the application.

Writing AngularJS application that make use of other modules/libraries is easy once you understand how to wrap them into a service and notify AngularJS that a model has changed.

Socket.io is probably one of the coolest things to come out of JavaScript world in recent years. Something that let web developers create real-time applications without the fuss of thinking about web sockets and long polling and all the other hacks that need to be used.

The idea is pretty much simple, the server can emit an event and the client will pick it up. Socket.io takes care of deciding which of the real-time hacks should be used to make the magic happen.

www.ingramcontent.com/pod-product-compliance
Lightning Source LLC
Chambersburg PA
CBHW060934050326
40689CB00013B/3093